AUSTRAL EDEN

200 years of Australian architecture

AUSTRAL EDEN

200 years of Australian architecture

PATRICK BINGHAM-HALL

The Watermark Press

For Tom, Val and Penny.
From Flat G to 55 Alexandra Street,
my first family and always my
greatest support.

First published in 1999 by
The Watermark Press,
Sydney, Australia

National Library of Australia
Cataloguing-in-Publication data

Bingham-Hall, Patrick.
    Austral Eden : 200 years of Australian architecture.

    Bibliography.
    Includes index.
    ISBN 0 949284 42 4.

    1. Architecture - Australia - History.
    2. Architecture - Australia - Pictorial works. I. Title.

720.994

Designed by Anna Stephen
Printed in China by South China Printing, Hong Kong

Contents

Swanston Street, Melbourne is now closed to traffic and known as Swanston Street Walk, although pedestrians need to be wary of the trams which still rumble through and the occasional semi-comic busker. The block between Collins Street and Bourke Street is pretty dingy, despite continual grand plans to brighten it up with colourful sculptures, outdoor cafes, and flower stalls. Every large city has one of these precincts - the office space is defiantly low-rent, young men on skateboards wheel around the greasy footpaths, and the local police maintain a conspicuous presence. A recently renovated shopping arcade and cinema complex, with nasty marble-look tiles and tacky light fittings is halfway along the western side of this block. If you make a few complicated arrangements in advance, and demonstrate sufficient credibility, you are met at the entrance to the arcade by the caretaker. He leads you up some badly-carpeted stairs, across a dark deserted lobby, through some doors and then up one more flight of stairs. It is now completely dark - the filtered sounds of city traffic are a constant background noise, and nesting pigeons that have been disturbed flap madly overhead. The caretaker fumbles around, finally locates the light-switch, and there it is. Resplendent, untouched, and hardly ever seen, the fantastic ceiling of the Capitol Theatre by Walter Burley Griffin and Marion Mahony, is lit up above you. A frozen moment of architectural genius.

Yes, there is architecture this good in Australia, and *Austral Eden* contains two hundred years of antipodean architectural highlights. The great colonial architect John Verge, retired to the Macleay Valley near Kempsey after seven years practice in Sydney, and named his large land grant 'Austral Eden'. Verge's best house at Camden Park, was built in 1834, and is an early example of skilled adaptation of prevailing architectural styles to local conditions. A Palladian mansion set in the rolling hills south-west of Sydney, Camden Park shows both Verge's Regency training and the already established specific requirements of Australian country houses. Australia's early architects were all trained in England, and given an opportunity in the expanding colony to build on a scale not possible back home. There was no real call in Britain for parliament houses, government houses, courthouses and cathedrals, certainly nothing to compare with the one thousand public buildings designed by James Barnet between 1862 and 1890. Many early Australian buildings were an inevitable transportation of London style and taste without alteration, and some of these were accomplished and worthy edifices, frequently enhanced by the use of local stone. However, the best architects - Greenway, Wardell, Blacket, Reed, Clark, and Barnet, all relished the possibilities given them, and in their finest moments designed buildings that were the equal of any in the world. The Gothic essays of Blacket and Wardell outshone the work of their mentor, Pugin, especially Wardell with St Patrick's Cathedral and the ES&A Bank, both in Melbourne. As in the United States, Canada, India, and other countries experiencing rapid colonization and settlement, the occasional provincial masterpiece was to appear. The magnificent Court House at Goulburn, and the Customs House on the banks of the wide brown Fitzroy River at Rockhampton, are most splendid evocations of the glorious far-flung British Empire.

9

Brilliant migrant architects were to arrive continually over the years, usually early in their careers, and produced their best work in Australia. John Horbury Hunt was the first notable example of a maverick, dogmatic architect who disembarked, in his case from Boston, with ideas, talents and self-conviction firmly in place. Hunt's uncompromising houses and churches, beautifully crafted from brick and timber, remain as monuments to the sound of a different drum. Two fellow Americans, Walter Burley Griffin and his wife Marion Mahony, arrived from Chicago after winning the design competition for Australia's capital city in 1912. Their architecture was as unconventional and eccentric as their personalities - Newman College and the Capitol Theatre, both in Melbourne, survive as spectacular testaments to their ingenuity and imagination. Their fascination with the Australian bush led to the remarkable houses of Castlecrag, which were built from Walter's patented 'Knitlock' concrete construction system. Frederick Romberg came to Australia in 1938, fleeing the rise of fascism, and was followed by Harry Seidler, escaping its aftermath in 1947. These two men were highly trained modern architects, and their sophisticated sculptural strengths were to flourish in Australia. Romberg's masterpiece of plastic expression was Stanhill Apartments built in Melbourne in 1948, and Seidler's prolific career began in 1950 with a small white box, a house for his mother in the bush of Sydney's North Shore. Australian-born architects were thriving by now, and men such as Robin Boyd, Roy Grounds, Neville Gruzman and Peter Muller were appropriating international architectural styles and adapting them to the sprawling Australian cities. Occasionally brilliant and original architects such as Oribin, Symonds, Buhrich, Iwanoff & Fombertaux illuminated the suburbs with wonderful idiosyncratic houses. The most interesting and spirited work came from the adaptation of foreign architecture converging with the continuing development of a local vernacular style.

Local climatic imperative and frequently impoverished financial circumstances had led to the initial Australianization of imported architecture and architects. Verandahs had immediately garlanded the first houses, and deep colonnades and arcades appeared on public buildings made from stone. The further north you travelled the more obvious this became. The buildings of Charters Towers require a lot more shade and ventilation than those of Warrnambool, and the first simple structures of the outback and the tropics were to provide rudimentary shelter and protection from the harsh environment. The cheapest materials were used, leading to a ubiquitous structure built from timber and tin. Embellishment and decoration followed, and a gradual metamorphosis from practical prosaic structure to inventive lyrical architecture was under way. The Moree Lands Department of 1896 was an elevated timber building with large verandahs, and coming from the office of the NSW Government Architect, Walter Vernon, shows sophisticated decorative design skills. This was one of the first outback public buildings made from timber and tin rather than stone, and shows architectural awareness of the specific local requirements of elevation, ventilation, and shade. Robin Dods applied an Arts and Crafts training in London and Edinburgh to a further refinement of Australian construction to produce sub-tropical architecture that is a picturesque expression of functional integrity. A similar combination of trained design skill and functional pragmatism is seen in the best houses of Harold Desbrowe-Annear.

The grafting of applied architectural erudition to practical vernacular development flowered soon after World War II. Australian architects adapted the organic planning and respectful use of materials shown in traditional Japanese architecture and the prairie houses of Frank Lloyd Wright to suburban houses in the bush. This evolved into the now celebrated Sydney School of the early sixties, where architects such as Ken Woolley built rugged romantic houses embracing their rough bushland sites. The C B Alexander Agricultural College at Tocal in 1965 by Ian McKay and Philip Cox is the revered monument to the crafted styling of this period. A spectacular and highly-principled fusion of architectural urbanity, environmental respect, and appropriate use of materials has followed in the work of such architects as Glenn Murcutt, Rick Leplastrier, and Gabriel Poole. This convergence of local and imported forms and theories has not been confined to houses in the bush. Invigorating expressive, experimental architecture has followed its own path through the suburbs of Melbourne since the early fifties, leading from Boyd, Grounds, and McIntyre to Denton Corker Marshall, Nonda Katsalidis, and Peter Corrigan.

The architectural history of any country or civilization is only known through its best works, 'always look up' is the fundamental instruction to any architectural tourist. Focus on the noble pursuits, the structural strengths, the classical cornices and ignore the shopfront alterations, the suburban sprawls and the miasma of contemporary corporate architecture. The ineptitude of Australian town-planning and poll-driven suburban housing (give them what they think they want) is the subject of another book. *Austral Eden* is a collection of Australian architectural gems - a demonstration of the evolution of heterogeneous regional architecture proud of its vernacular origins, imported forms and theories, stylistic freedom and indigenous respect. For such a sparsely populated country, we've done pretty well, and in two hundred years - not bad at all.

1788-1865

Arcadian Visions in the Australian Bush

Virtually untouched since 1820, the original villages of Tasmania, strung along the narrow plain between Hobart and Launceston, remain romantic evocations of colonial Australia. These settlements containing hotels, churches, simple Georgian cottages, and a gaol, were simply English country villages built in the antipodean wilderness. Tasmania, previously known as Van Diemen's Land, is about as antipodean as you can get, and the image of Chipping Campden landed in the wilderness, though picturesque, is quite unsettling. The architecture of the public buildings reflects both the desire to transplant English aesthetic ideals, and the need to reinforce colonial power and authority. The parish church of St. Luke's in Richmond shows this paradox, a simple elegant Gothic church backed by rolling hills, but it was designed by a military engineer and there is an austerity and sternness of proportion expected in a penal colony.

Early colonial settlement was restricted to New South Wales and Tasmania, until the founding of Melbourne in 1835. In New South Wales, small stone villages were established where land was cleared for farming. Some of these inland villages, such as Berrima and Hartley, displayed an arcadian vision with classical Greek courthouses surrounded by forests of gumtrees. Sydney's early architecture was rudimentary, enhanced briefly by the enlightenment of Governor Macquarie and the shooting star of Francis Greenway, an architect from Bristol, convicted of forgery and transported to Australia in 1814. His best work has an originality and sophistication that must have been quite a sight in the scruffy ramshackle colony of 1824.

The first large houses and homesteads were basically adaptations of standard English models, often taken from pattern-books, with the immediate incorporation of the verandah. This climatic necessity was the first tangible expression of a local architecture. The early unsophisticated colonial architecture was superseded by the more fashionable and expensive Regency style in the 1830s. The great architect of this period was John Verge, and his masterpiece was Camden Park House, a Palladian villa in the hills south of Sydney.

13

Gold was discovered in 1851, Melbourne became boom town Australia, and boom buildings were needed. Enter such men as Joseph Reed, William Wardell and J J Clark, whose mastery of Neo-Renaissance forms and proportions transformed the straggly village on the banks of the Yarra into Marvellous Melbourne. The suburbs and small farming communities that grew up around Sydney could now be identified by the Puginesque spires of Edmund Blacket, who also designed the first massive buildings for Sydney University.

The convict settlements and colonial port towns were becoming cities, and the architecture was to demonstrate the prosperity and optimism of the Victorian age. However, the most romantic and inspirational architecture from this early period is to be found in the small pioneering villages, where classical forms and idealistic visions were hardened by the harsh realities of a lonely and unpleasant existence on the other side of the world.

HYDE PARK BARRACKS Sydney, NSW 1817-1819 Architect – Francis Greenway

A monumental dormitory for convicts designed by a convict, who was pardoned on the building's completion. Francis Greenway was Australia's first great architect, and this unpretentious structure with its elegant proportions and robust presence is Australia's first great building.

HAMBLEDON COTTAGE Parramatta, Sydney, NSW 1822

One of three remaining early farmhouses in Parramatta, where Australian farming began. Now surrounded by Sydney's suburban sprawl, this humble homestead shows the adaptation of English rural architecture to local conditions with a broad verandah and low-slung roof.

ST MATTHEW'S Windsor, NSW 1817-1823 Architect – Francis Greenway
Perched on the ridge overlooking the Hawkesbury River and the Blue Mountains, a perfectly
proportioned church with urns borrowed from Sir John Soane.

ST LUKE'S Richmond, Tas 1834 Architect – John Lee Archer
The English parish church in the wilds of Van Diemen's Land. The landscape has been
tamed and the scene has a pastoral peacefulness worthy of Wensleydale.

ELIZABETH BAY HOUSE Sydney, NSW 1837 Architect – John Verge
The grandest house in the colony with an elliptical double-storey vestibule and views the length of
Sydney Harbour, built for the Colonial Secretary, Alexander MacLeay.

19

CAMDEN PARK HOUSE Camden, NSW 1835 Architect – John Verge
Designed for the Macarthur family on a hill overlooking the pastures of Camden and Menangle, Camden Park House is a
masterpiece of Palladian refinement from an accomplished but reluctant architect, who retired to Austral Eden in 1837.

ROSS BRIDGE Ross, Tas 1836 Architect – John Lee Archer
Archer was a trained architect who had worked with the London Bridge
designer, John Rennie, and here in central Tasmania built a stone bridge
whose grace and symmetry belie its constructional pragmatism.

BERRIMA COURT HOUSE Berrima, NSW 1838 Architect – Mortimer Lewis
An arcadian vision in the Australian bush, a Greek temple for convicting sheep thieves and bushrangers.

ST GEORGE'S Hobart, Tas 1836-1841 Architect – John Lee Archer and James Blackburn
A navigational and spiritual aid to sailors entering the Derwent River, the tower by Blackburn above
an Archer nave was whimsically inspired by the Tower of Winds in Athens.

ST MATTHEW'S Rokeby, Tas 1839-1843 Architect – James Blackburn

A humble Gothic church with a lack of pretension and adornment, conveying the bleakness
and the austerity of the early years in Tasmania.

ST MARK'S Pontville, Tas 1839 Architect – James Blackburn

A charming, if somewhat naïve parish church with a Romanesque arch and two rising
arcades indicating stairs, which do not exist.

ST ANDREW'S Strathalbyn, SA 1851 Builder – English & Brown Brothers
Strathalbyn is an English country village in the Australian bush, with stone pubs,
duckponds, a village green and a parish church.

CORIO VILLA Geelong. Vic 1856

The cast-iron pieces, roofing iron, and classic vases which make up this house were shipped from Glasgow to Geelong in 1855. They remained unclaimed for six months, until sold to a local businessman. Local craftsmen constructed Corio Villa without plans or directions.

FORT DENISON Sydney Harbour, NSW 1855-1857 Engineer – George Barney

A sandstone fort with a Martello tower built on Pinchgut Island to protect Sydney from the Russians.

PARLIAMENT HOUSE Melbourne, Vic 1856 Architect – Knight & Kerr

With its great flight of steps and massive Roman Doric colonnade, this monumental edifice is still capable of
demonstrating the power of the state to citizens of Melbourne.

MAIN QUADRANGLE BUILDING Sydney University, NSW 1854-1859 Architect – Edmund Blacket
The architect was commissioned to design the first buildings of Sydney University in the established medieval Gothic style of Oxford and
Cambridge. On a commanding site just west of the city, Blacket supplied the dreaming spires that were required.

CLARENDON TERRACE East Melbourne, Vic 1857 Architect – Osgood Pritchard

John Nash would have been proud. In a settlement barely 20 years old, this Corinthian terrace
would not have been out of place in Regents Park, London.

HODGKINSON HOUSE East Melbourne, Vic 1861 Architect – Joseph Reed
A domestic Gothic townhouse remarkable for the contrast between the decorative
timberwork of the verandahs and the sombre bluestone walls.

ST PATRICK'S CATHEDRAL Melbourne, Vic 1861 Architect – William Wardell
One of the great cathedrals of the 19th century, with three soaring sandstone spires rising
above the bluestone chapels clustered below.

TREASURY BUILDING Melbourne, Vic 1862 Architect – J J Clark
An elegant and perfectly proportioned Renaissance palazzo for counting gold.
J J Clark was only 19 when he signed the plans for this building.

CASTLEMAINE MARKET Castlemaine, Vic 1861-62 Architect – William Beynon Downe

A remarkably refined provincial market building designed by the town surveyor, who had obviously studied his Wren and Jones.

The old Police Station in the Rocks area of Sydney is a small sandstone composition built in 1882 bursting with mannerist vigour and energy. Incorporating at least half the classical forms found in an architectural dictionary, it is but one of a thousand buildings designed by James Barnet, a formidable Scotsman and New South Wales Colonial Architect from 1862 to 1890. Barnet's best buildings were an inventive monumental implementation of the classical forms of High Victorian architecture, and have a unique beauty and resonance due to the use of honey-coloured Sydney sandstone.

Many of the buildings of the period between the Gold Rush and the Depression of the 1890s were spectacular expressions of civic and personal pride. The landmark buildings of most country towns — the post offices, court houses, and town halls were nearly all built at this time, and are eclectic highly decorated set-pieces, usually in the Italianate style. The most prolific architects in the two largest cities were Joseph Reed, William Wardell, Edmund Blacket, and Barnet. All were exceptionally facile architects, who switched from style to style as fashion determined, particularly Reed who was perhaps too eclectic, he never made any style his own, and his work now seems relatively ephemeral. Wardell's best work, like that of Barnet, appears far more substantial, and the E S & A (now ANZ) Bank on the corner of Queen and Collins Streets in Melbourne is one of the most beautiful commercial buildings of the time to be seen anywhere.

Individual stylists surfaced throughout Australia, William Pitt in Melbourne, George Addison in Brisbane, Frederick Menkens in Newcastle, George McRae in Sydney and the peripatetic J J Clark. Much of the architecture was sheer flamboyance and extravagance, with little concession to local landscape and climate. It was a period of Baroque indulgence. Some architects, though, were following their own separate, more stylistically rigorous paths, and can now be seen as precursors to modernism. Chief among these was the American *arriviste*, John Horbury Hunt, who marched to the sound of a different drum, and was openly contemptuous of all architectural sham and hypocrisy. His knowledge of construction in brick and timber combined with a utilitarian approach to a building's function produced some powerful and resolute churches and houses. Another architect showing ornamental restraint and a practical attitude to the usefulness of a building was William Kemp, Architect for Schools in New South Wales.

Further north, a humble start was being made in the development of an appropriate architecture for a tropical climate. The timber and tin vernacular was already being employed for sound structural and economic reasons, and this would soon evolve into genuine architecture. Simple though decorative timber churches, and wooden houses raised on stilts were already appearing. The Victorian period, though, will remain the age of magnificent mansions built from gold, Baroque mercantile extravagance, and mannerist monuments carved from stone.

MORTUARY STATION Redfern, Sydney, NSW 1868 Architect – James Barnet
Funeral trains left this sombre sandstone station, a rare exercise in the Gothic
style by James Barnet, for another at the Rookwood Necropolis.

BERRIMA GAOL Berrima, NSW 1866 Architect – James Barnet
Those who passed regularly through this portal may not have fully appreciated its beautiful honey-coloured stonework.

BISHOPSBOURNE Milton, Brisbane, Qld 1865-1868 Architect – Benjamin Backhouse
Surrounded by wide verandahs with Gothic arches, this home to Anglican Archbishops until 1964
has a distinctly Australian though ecclesiastical character.

BROUGHAM PLACE UNITING CHURCH North Adelaide, SA 1860-72 Architect – Wright & Woods and G & E Hamilton
A serene presence on the slopes of North Adelaide, gazing benignly over the city of churches.

HOLYROOD Strathfield, Sydney, NSW 1873 Architect – G & R Mansfield
Previously the City Bank in Sydney, this Italianate edifice was moved to Strathfield
after being damaged by fire, and installed as the entrance to a rather large family home.

ST STEPHEN'S Newtown, Sydney, NSW 1871-74 Architect – Edmund Blacket

With its crumbling stonework and overgrown cemetery providing elegiac opportunities for inner-west wordsmiths, this is the finest of all
Blacket's churches, distinguished by a slender spritely spire.

RIPPONLEA Elsternwick, Melbourne, Vic 1876 Architect – Reed and Barnes
Paradise in Elsternwick. Surrounded by lakes, lawns, a fernery and a grotto, this mansion features
the polychrome brickwork much favoured by Joseph Reed at the time.

AYERS HOUSE Adelaide. SA 1858-1874 Architect – George Strickland Kingston

A house built in several stages, beginning with a single-storey central cottage, to which Kingston added
his trademark arched porches and grand bow-fronted rooms

GOVERNMENT HOUSE Melbourne, Vic 1876 Architect – William Wardell
A resplendent vice-regal residence with a balustraded tower only ever glimpsed by
locals through the trees of the Royal Botanic Gardens or from low flying aeroplanes.

PALM HOUSE Botanic Gardens, Adelaide, SA 1876 Designed by Gustav Runge
Prefabricated in Germany, this glasshouse is a rare surviving Australian example of
the advances made at this time in iron and glass construction.

49

ST GEORGE'S Beenleigh, Brisbane, Qld 1876 Architect – F D G Stanley
This simple church with an exposed timber structure now lives in a retirement home
for old buildings in the southern Brisbane suburbs.

50

WERRIBEE PARK MANSION Werribee, Vic 1878 Architect – J H Fox
The first palace of the squattocracy, a fifty room mansion set amongst rose gardens, sweeping lawns, ponds, grottoes and a zoo.

ST CLAIRE Hunters Hill, Sydney, NSW 1879 Architect – Charles Jeanneret

Overlooking the Parramatta River rather than the Seine, this fine sandstone house with a delicate iron lace verandah screen
is one of many designed in Hunters Hill by French settlers.

ST GEORGE'S St Kilda, Melbourne, Vic 1877-1880 Architect – Albert Purchas

Remarkable for a beautiful banded bell-tower, much loved by local muezzins, St George's of St Kilda is a characteristic Romanesque
Gothic design by Albert Purchas, whose churches decorate much of Victoria and southern NSW.

THE BOTANIC HOTEL Adelaide, SA 1877 Architect – M McMullen
A perfectly regulation hotel building on the eastern corner of North Terrace wearing
her three verandahs as hooped skirts.

SOUTH MELBOURNE TOWN HALL South Melbourne, Vic 1880 Architect – Charles Webb

Viewed across its parade ground, this is the most imposing and commanding of the monumental town halls
built in the inner Melbourne suburbs at the time.

ST PAUL'S CATHEDRAL Melbourne. Vic 1880-1891 Architect – William Butterfield   1931 – James Barr (spires)

With its gateway position opposite Flinders Street Station and Federation Square, St Pauls' Gothic massing determines the visual context
for much of Melbourne, despite being designed in London, with towers arriving fifty years later from a Sydney architect.

BOURKE STREET SCHOOL Surry Hills, Sydney, NSW 1883 Architect – William Kemp
William Kemp designed a number of distinctive schools at this time, featuring two wings – boys on the left,
girls on the right, and a central entrance with a tower.

CARCOAR COURT HOUSE Carcoar, NSW 1882 Architect – James Barnet

An Italianate style courthouse for the town that time forgot. A Blacket spire rises in the background.

MORTUARY CHAPEL Maryborough, Qld 1884 Architect – Willoughby Powell

A drive-through chapel for horse-drawn hearses, with a tower whose vaguely suggestive profile was hopefully not remarked upon by 19th century mourners.

CHRIST CHURCH CATHEDRAL Grafton, NSW 1874-1884 Architect – John Horbury Hunt

With its masterly brickwork, expressive entrance arch, and absence of Victorian affectation, this powerful original
work anticipates many of the trends of the next fifty years in architecture.

ANZ (Formerly E S & A) BANK Melbourne, Vic 1884 Architect – William Wardell
An elegant exercise in Venetian Gothic notable for its restraint at a time of
ubiquitous High Victorian ornamental encrustation.

BENDIGO TOWN HALL Bendigo, Vic 1885 Architect – W C Vahland

Bendigo was the biggest boom town of all, and this *hotel de ville* demonstrates the flamboyance, pomp, and self belief of the period. Once again, somebody forgot the clock.

EARP GILLAM BOND STORE Newcastle, NSW 1888 Architect – Frederick Menkens

A colourful and robust warehouse by Frederick Menkens from Oldenburg, who arrived in Australia in 1876 and
set up practice in Newcastle in 1882. His adaptation of northern European architecture to Australian conditions
and requirements has left Newcastle with some unique warehouses, churches and office buildings.

ST PATRICK'S SEMINARY Manly, Sydney, NSW 1885 Architect – Sheerin & Hennessy
Crowning the hill above Manly, and best viewed from a surfboard, St Patrick's grim Gothic presence
is a reminder of the choices one makes in life.

BOOLOOMINBAH Armidale, NSW 1887 Architect – John Horbury Hunt

A massive mansion with a spectacular arrangement of forms and textures that have their own logic and rhythm.

GOULBURN COURT HOUSE Goulburn, NSW 1888 Architect – James Barnet

The most splendiferous of all Barnet's courthouses, a triumphant work from an architect who, with his thousand
or so public buildings across NSW, supplied a sense of civic pride and spirit that will never be replaced.

HUNTER BAILLIE CHURCH Annandale, Sydney, NSW 1888 Architect – Cyril and Arthur Blacket
The tallest of the Blacket ring of spires surrounding inner Sydney, and the only one designed by Edmund's sons.

STOCK EXCHANGE ARCADE Charters Towers, Qld 1888 Architect – M C Day

Originally designed as an arcade with two floors of shops and offices, this glazed vault supported by steel trusses was
taken over by the Stock Exchange at the height of the Charters Towers Gold Rush.

EULALIA Norman Park, Brisbane, Qld 1889 Architect – Hunter and Corrie

As befitting a democratic city without a best suburb, every Brisbane suburb has a collection of best houses.

The best houses sit on the hills, not in the valleys, and Eulalia certainly sits on a hill.

THE MANSIONS Brisbane, Qld 1889 Architect – G H M Addison

Previously chief draftsman for Melbourne firm Terry and Oakden, and close friend of artist Tom Roberts, George Addison arrived in
Brisbane in 1886. His flamboyant and exuberant style made an immediate impression, and The Mansions with its shady arcaded verandahs
is typical of his adaptation of High-Victorian style to sub-tropical conditions.

CUSTOMS HOUSE Brisbane, Qld 1885-1889 Architect – Charles McLay

It may be fanciful to suggest that the unexpected curves and projections of this building echo those of the meandering Brisbane River, but
this sub-tropical baroque would look out of place in any other city.

TREASURY BUILDING Brisbane, Qld 1885-1888 Architect – J J Clark
Subsequently revered as a masterpiece of Mid-Victorian Renaissance design, J J Clark designed the Treasury Building in Melbourne twenty
five years earlier. This Brisbane version is perhaps the most sumptuous and assured of all Australian classical Victorian buildings.

A C GOODE HOUSE Melbourne, Vic 1891 Architect – Wright, Reed & Beaver
A Gothic birdhouse carved out of sandstone that provides a still potent image of Marvellous Melbourne.

ILLAWARRA Toorak, Melbourne, Vic 1889 Architect – James Birtwhistle
The classic Toorak mansion, now somewhat incongruously surrounded by Neo-Georgian nouveau riche.
Note the fanned bracket supporting the circular balcony.

OLDERFLEET BUILDING (left) and **RIALTO BUILDINGS** (above) Melbourne. Vic 1889 Architect – William Pitt
William Pitt provided the bookends to Collins Street's fabulous set of richly decorated mercantile buildings. Both
the Olderfleet and the Rialto are in Venetian Gothic style, and the overall effect recalls Bruges
or Antwerp, with the Rialto Building tipping its hat to Norman Shaw.

Former QUEENSLAND MUSEUM Brisbane, Qld 1891 Architect – G H M Addison
A wilful exercise in Byzantine Gothic, completed just in time for the financial crash of the early nineties.
We didn't see much Byzantine Gothic after that.

MELVILLE MEMORIAL Maryborough, Qld 1889

Imported from Scotland after being selected at the Glasgow Exhibition as most suitable for the banks
of the Mary River, this rotunda originally housed a fountain.

JOHN STREET PUBLIC SCHOOL Pyrmont, Sydney, NSW 1891 Architect – William Kemp
Not a gargoyle to be seen. A dignified building clearly showing the movement away from ornamental and
eclectic revivalism to structural and functional integrity.

JOHN TAYLOR WAREHOUSE Pyrmont, Sydney, NSW 1893 Architect – Arthur Blacket
With thinly applied decorative archwork, the most elegant surviving Pyrmont woolstore.

LABASSA Caulfield, Melbourne, Vic 1889-91 Architect – J A B Koch
Built just before the financial crash of 1892, this hidden gem in suburban Caulfield is the final
baroque flourish of boom-style flamboyance and voluptuousness.

HIGHLANDS Waitara, Sydney, NSW 1893 Architect – John Horbury Hunt
One of a series of shingled mansions designed by Hunt between 1888 and 1893, and a brooding essay in a style that
was to become popular twenty years later surrounding the golf courses of affluent suburbs.

ST ANDREW'S Manly, Sydney, NSW 1892 Architect – Sulman and Power

A formidable stone church by Sulman in the massive Romanesque style which never became
popular in Australia for obvious climatic reasons.

QUEEN VICTORIA BUILDING Sydney, NSW 1893-98 Architect – George McRae

Representing a final flourish of Victorian architectural indulgence, this recently restored market place with a relentless
repetition of arches, columns, and copper domes would be inconceivable built in anything but Sydney sandstone.

AIR FORCE CLUB Newcastle, NSW 1892 Architect – Frederick Menkens

Commerce looks over the Port of Newcastle from her plinth in the gable of Menkens' masterpiece.

CHRIST CHURCH CATHEDRAL Newcastle, NSW 1895 Architect – John Horbury Hunt

The volatile architect was sacked from the job in 1895, twenty five years after winning the initial design competition. Dominating the city skyline, the cathedral was finally completed in 1979 and is a dramatic testament to the power and originality of Hunt's work.

SOUTH BRISBANE TOWN HALL South Brisbane, Qld 1892 Architect - John Hall & Son

A resounding manifestation of local pride, an elaborate campanile making a defiant gesture to the city across the river.

NATIONAL AUSTRALIA BANK Brisbane, Qld 1895 Architect - F D G Stanley
Colonial prosperity writ large in the prevailing classical manner. Still dominating central Brisbane
despite conceding thirty or forty floors to its rivals

From the balcony of the Chadwick house, on the slopes of the Heidelberg hills, Arthur Streeton's view to the Dandenongs over the Yarra Valley is framed by the large timber eyes of Harold Desbrowe-Annear. "The eyes of the house look out on the world", said Harold, and these eyes gaze forever over the gliding stream. The Chadwick house is one of three by Desbrowe-Annear stepping down the hillside in a residential subdivision then known as the Eaglemont estate. This was an initial attempt to establish a complementary and aesthetically rewarding relationship with the environment, specifically the Australian bush. Desbrowe-Annear's three houses used an organic approach to form redolent of the Arts and Crafts movement with lyrical curves, stained timber, and insistent integration with the garden and the view.

This house is not entirely consistent with the oeuvre of Desbrowe-Annear, as he lost his touch in Toorak, but it clearly symbolizes the progression from Victorian stylistic ostentation to a more evocative site-specific architecture. More constant in application and development was Robin Dods, one of the quiet heroes of Australian architectural history. Dods introduced spacious well-ventilated timber houses with wide verandahs and elegant curvaceous timber-work to the suburbs of sub-tropical Brisbane. Across outback and tropical Australia, the principles of cross-ventilation and structural elevation were now being applied to public buildings and large houses, always adorned with large shady verandahs.

Following the excesses of the High-Victorian age, this was a transitional period in Australian architecture, shattered by the Great War. Some localized, idiosyncratic talents flowered briefly, and some highly original public buildings sprang from the drawing boards of the Government Architects in Brisbane and Sydney. Monumental buildings in the classical style were still taking shape, lending civic gravitas to provincial centres. The Rockhampton Customs House and the Newcastle Post Office are two of the most refined and resplendent neo-classical edifices in the country. A hybrid housing style, now rather apathetically referred to as 'Federation', was taking over the suburbs of the large cities. Fusing Art Nouveau decoration with the picturesque massing and proportions of the Queen Anne style, the ubiquitous Federation house had its occasional dramatic moments. 'Carclew' in North Adelaide and 'Dalswraith' in Kew, Melbourne, being most notable.

The practical and unpretentious timber buildings of outback Queensland were becoming more architecturally sophisticated. The structurally honest method of using the exposed timber frame for decorative purpose is displayed by the elaborate wooden Gothic church of St Mary's, Beaudesert, and the intricate baroque tower of the Range Convent in Rockhampton. This transformation from pragmatic, vernacular structure to unique regional architecture is also seen in Charters Towers, where the Boer War Memorial, a sublime assemblage of curving tinplate and cast-iron framework, is a dignified and expressive monument to the folly of imperial heroism.

PERTH OBSERVATORY Perth, WA 1896 Architect - George Temple Poole
Superintendent of Public Works in Perth from 1885 to 1896, George Temple Poole designed a number of buildings still emblematic of the
city. The Observatory reflects the stylistic retreat of the late 1890s, a public building that could be mistaken for a house.

FORMER SUBIACO INDUSTRIAL COLLEGE Perth, WA 1896 Architect – George Temple Poole with Robert Haddon
An early and exuberant work by Robert Haddon, who later refined his style in Melbourne.

TITLES OFFICE Perth, WA 1897 Architect – George Temple Poole
With two floors of colonnaded overhanging balconies, this building is a spectacular sight in the decidedly less than picturesque Perth business district.

MEERILINGA Perth, WA 1897

Witches' hats were popular at the time, and this one comes with a slender ribbed chimney and a palindromic verandah.

94

ST JAMES Menangle, NSW 1898 Architect – John Sulman

Erected by Elizabeth Macarthur-Onslow in memory of her husband and parents on the hill overlooking the Macarthur
estate at Camden Park. A romantic and slightly indulgent work by a mannered and eclectic architect.

CARCLEW North Adelaide, SA 1897 Architect – John Quinton Bruce
Only the best money could have built it, and only a rather large pile of architectural adjectives could describe it.

WATSON HOUSE Maryborough, Qld circa 1898

Maryborough is renowned for its large elaborate timber houses, or Queenslanders as they are known, and this is
a splendid example of the Queenslander that most Queenslanders dream of.

LANDS DEPARTMENT Moree, NSW 1893-96 (Rebuilt after fire 1980) Architect - Walter Liberty Vernon
A light and graceful structure which marks a new awareness of the need for shade and ventilation in the outback.

SHAMROCK HOTEL Bendigo, Vic 1897 Architect – Kennedy & Hutton
A legendary hotel. Forever the symbol of provincial Victorian wealth.

WARWICK POST OFFICE Warwick, Qld 1899 Architect – A B Brady with Thomas Pye
Mannerist whimsy in sandstone, with keyhole arches on the upper verandah giving a vaguely
Moorish feel to the main street of a busy country town.

BURNETT RIVER BRIDGE Bundaberg. Qld 1900 Architect – A B Brady

Following disastrous floods in 1893, Alfred Brady in his role as Queensland Government Architect and Engineer for Bridges had to
construct new, indestructible bridges in Brisbane, Bundaberg, and Maryborough. This Bundaberg structure,
prosaically described as of hog-back lattice girder design, is in fact a remarkably lyrical river crossing with a
serpentine upper deck supported by three sets of piers with ingenious circular bracing.

COMMERCIAL HOTEL Rockhampton, Qld 1898 Architect – John William Wilson

Mythical Queensland is full of pubs like this, in real Queensland they have mostly disappeared.

102

LADY LAMINGTON NURSES HOME Royal Brisbane Hospital, Brisbane, Qld 1897 Architect - Hall and Dods
With its simple rhythmic forms, elegant proportions and shady verandahs, this competition-winning design
introduced Robin Dods to Brisbane architecture.

ARCHER PARK RAILWAY STATION Rockhampton. Qld 1899 Architect – Henrik Hansen
Trains still roll down the middle of the street in Rockhampton, and Archer Park was the central station for the various
rail networks which converge on the town. The station is also notable for its arched roof over the platforms.

DAVID COHEN BOND STORE Newcastle, NSW 1901 Architect – Frederick Menkens

A monumental facade with beautiful brick detailing and an overall compositional strength which suggests
that Menkens was one of Australia's most accomplished virtuoso architects.

SPRINGTHORPE MEMORIAL Booroondarah Cemetery, Kew, Melbourne, Vic 1897-1900 Architect – Harold Desbrowe-Annear
A Doric temple with polished black granite columns containing a Pre-Raphaelite tableau illuminated by a red skylight.

NEWCASTLE POST OFFICE Newcastle. NSW 1903 Architect – Walter Liberty Vernon
Vernon succeeded the prolific James Barnet as the NSW Government Architect in 1890, and for the next
twenty years continued a remarkable tradition of monumental individual designs for public buildings of all types.
This post office is a Palladian sandstone symbol of Novocastian pride at the turn of the century.

CUSTOMS HOUSE Rockhampton, Qld 1901 Architect – A B Brady with Thomas Pye
Bramante on the Fitzroy, the crowning glory of a golden period in Queensland public architecture.

108

ST BRIGID'S Townsville, Qld 1904 Architect – Doig and Ritchie
A tropical application of Gothic parish church design resulting in a timber building far
more lyrical and charming than any stone counterpart. Note the flying buttresses.

IMPERIAL HOTEL Ravenswood, Qld 1902
A surreal pub in a ghost town that has inevitably become the
backdrop for a thousand beer advertisements.

CHADWICK HOUSE Eaglemont, Melbourne, Vic 1903 Architect – Harold Desbrowe-Annear
"The eyes of the house look out on the world" claimed Harold Desbrowe-Annear,
and he gave this house a pair of large timber spectacles.

CREMORNE Hamilton, Brisbane, Qld 1905 Architects – Eaton & Bates
Hamilton's house on the hill is not so much a house as a collection of bandstands
with a sweeping view over the Brisbane River.

MIDDLE HALL, RANGE CONVENT Rockhampton, Qld 1907–1908 Architect – C Slater
Planned and inspired by Bishop James Duhig, later Archbishop of Brisbane, this spectacular timber tower
on the Athelstane Range above Rockhampton surmounts a large hall used for classrooms on the first floor.
Ten music rooms, a library, and rooms for photography, art, and cooking were on the ground floor.

ST MARY'S Beaudesert, Qld 1907 Architect – G H M Addison

An exercise by the remarkably adept Mr Addison in building what he termed "the massive
picturesque design of sacred edifices in older lands" with timber rather than stone.

CENTRAL RAILWAY STATION Sydney. NSW 1904-1908 Architect – Walter Liberty Vernon
A grand terminal redolent of the age. Now something of a honey-coloured white elephant, one can only pray
that its rusticated colonnade, massive booking hall and clock tower are treated with due respect.

ST ANDREW'S Brisbane. Qld 1902-1910 Architect – G D Payne

Taking a cue from Horbury Hunt, this church with its unadorned arches, bold massing, and perfect brickwork is a defiant example of early-modernist architecture.

DALSWRAITH Kew, Melbourne, Vic 1906 Architect – Ussher and Kemp
Emphatically marking the change in taste and style from boom-style mansions such as Labassa and Illawarra,
this Arts and Crafts home for draper William Gibson features steep gables and timbered bay windows.

WYLIE'S BATHS Coogee, Sydney, NSW 1907 Architect/Builder – H A Wylie 1993-95 – Renovations and Repairs – Allen Jack + Cottier
Tall timber, chequerboard cladding, a sun deck, and a rock pool combine to give vernacular Australian architecture a beatific Sydney home.

BABWORTH HOUSE Darling Point, Sydney, NSW 1909 Architect – Morrow and De Putron

Crowning the hill at Darling Point, Babworth House is a rather run-down mansion
with extensive art nouveau decoration and detailing.

BOER WAR MEMORIAL Charters Towers, Qld 1910 Architect – F Jorgensen
A cast iron and tinplate structure honouring 82 local men who fought in South Africa.
Reminiscent of a giant pith helmet, any symbolic reference is perhaps fanciful.

POLLARDS (now Fossey's) STORE Charters Towers, Qld 1909
An unlikely piece of outback whimsy with octagonal towers and an outsized arch hiding behind a zigzagged awning.

PALISADE HOTEL Millers Point, Sydney, NSW 1912 Design Engineer – Henry Walsh
With its somewhat surreal siting and aspect much loved by independent film-makers, this waterfront hotel has
a toughness and brutal honesty entirely in keeping with its clientele.

AML&F WOOLSTORE Teneriffe, Brisbane, Qld 1912 Architect – Hall & Dods
One of the few remaining examples of commercial work by Robin Dods, this woolstore has a sophisticated
visual impact with vertical lines of banded brickwork alternating with tall shallow-arched windows.

ERYLDENE Gordon, Sydney, NSW 1913 Architect – W Hardy Wilson

Surrounded by Professor E G Waterhouse's famous collection of camellias,
this house is a wistful revival of Colonial Georgian architecture.

125

TAMROOKUM CHAPEL Tamrookum, Qld 1915 Architect – Robin Dods
In this bucolic environment, the graceful sinuous lines of Dods mark the move from
architectural ostentation to natural harmony and climatic responsiveness.

Flowing down the hillside above Sydney's naval dockyard at Garden Island are the curving streamlined apartments of Wyldefel Gardens, built in 1936. Strolling through the central gardens of the terraced complex today is an exhilarating experience. The freshness and clarity of the crisp nautical forms are a white-painted evocation of the ambitions and idealism of the new modern architecture, when a democratic heroic vision could be realized in the age of the machine. Lines were simplified, shapes were purified, forms justified, and ornament removed. Streamlined horizontal architecture in Australia manifested itself most dramatically in hospitals, where the sheer white mass of the building wrapped with long bold bands of glass proved a dynamic expression of restorative cleanliness, and in factories where it symbolized speed and productivity.

The twenties and thirties saw the flowering of art-deco, a popular though ephemeral style rendered emotionally and symbolically powerful by Bruce Dellit and Emil Sodersten. Dellit's Anzac War Memorial in Sydney's Hyde Park is a deeply moving temple to the tragedy and pathos of colonial boys led to slaughter on the other side of the globe. The mythological imagery and Nietschean symbolism of art-deco adorned cinemas and department stores, often in combination with an exaggerated horizontality or verticality of structure in the form of blades, bands, or piers. This fashionable use of art-deco was tangible visible evidence of the beginning of the shift in popular culture from England to America; from London to Los Angeles in the age of the cinema.

A rarefied and uplifting form of American culture visited Australia in 1914, and stayed until 1936. Walter Burley Griffin won the competition for the design of the new capital city, Canberra, in 1912, and arrived two years later with his wife, Marion Mahony. This extraordinarily gifted and productive couple could be counted among the greatest and most eccentric architectural talents of the century.

The two volatile decades between the wars saw an awakening of national pride symbolized by the construction of the Sydney Harbour Bridge, a massive and magnificent structure that has become as emblematic of Australia as koalas and Bondi Beach. With varying degrees of credibility, flamboyant and eclectic designs for office buildings were erected, though attempted skyscrapers were foiled by city height limits. Melbourne, especially, has a rather cute streetscape of dwarf skyscrapers in the centre of the city, with some elegant distillations of the prevailing styles by Marcus Barlow and Harry Norris.

The emergence of modernism was the real story of architectural progress at the time, with most of the initial forays being essays in plain brickwork, relying on massing and conflicting planes for effect. The best examples were all in Melbourne; the uncompromising MacRobertson Girls High School, the Heidelberg Town Hall (worthy of Dudok himself) and the beautiful McPherson's Building. Melbourne also saw the arrival in 1938 of Frederick Romberg, whose urbane implementation of the International Style was the sign of things to come.

NEWMAN COLLEGE University Of Melbourne. Vic 1915-1918 Architect – Walter Burley Griffin and Marion Mahony

An anthroposophical anomaly, this is a building that one never really expects to see,
a mystical fantasy that defies architectural appellation.

129

EDINBURGH ROAD HOUSE Castlecrag, Sydney, NSW 1921 Architect – Walter Burley Griffin and Marion Mahony
Constructed in Knitlock, Griffin's own method of concrete block construction, this house is one of the first built by the Griffins in
Castlecrag, where they were integral in establishing a community lifestyle embracing anthroposophical
philosophies amidst the rugged rocky bush landscape of the Castlecrag peninsula.

CAPITOL THEATRE Melbourne, Vic 1921-24
Architect – Walter Burley Griffin and Marion Mahony
A truly psychedelic experience, a ceiling that must have inspired much
impatience as a dull movie delayed the lights being turned on again.

DENDY ST BATHING SHEDS Brighton, Melbourne, Vic 1920's
An endearing collection of brightly coloured bathing pavilions on Port Phillip Bay that will prove to be
a more enduring image of Melbourne's charm than any mile-high skyscraper.

CHURCH OF OUR LADY OF MT CARMEL AND ST PETER AND ST PAUL Mullewa. WA 1920-1923 Architect – Monsignor John C Hawes

Also known as Friar Jerome, Hawes built this romantic outback curiosity with his own hands. Trained in England, he built several churches in the
Bahamas and came to Australia as a missionary, where he constructed many eclectic Spanish Mission style churches,
including Geraldton Cathedral. He returned to the Bahamas in 1940 to live as a hermit.

CHURCH STREET BRIDGE Melbourne, Vic 1924 Architect – Harold Desbrowe-Annear and T R Ashworth

Linking Richmond with South Yarra, these three low arcaded reinforced concrete arches with lighting pylons are
a seductive manifestation of Desbrowe-Annear's ideas of the City Beautiful.

PHYSICS BUILDING Sydney University, NSW 1926 Architect – Leslie Wilkinson
Generally credited with popularizing the Mediterranean style in Sydney, Australia's first Professor of Architecture
designed this building in direct contrast to the pervasive Gothic style of the existing university.

MANCHESTER UNITY BUILDING Melbourne. Vic 1929-32 Architect – Marcus Barlow
A streamlined version of the Chicago Tribune Tower, enhanced by golden glazed
terracotta facing and a theatrical corner setting.

STATE THEATRE (Formerly Forum Theatre) Melbourne, Vic 1928 Architect – Bohringer Taylor & Johnson
A minaret on the corner of Russell and Flinders Streets, but nobody is fooled, this could only be a cinema. Seville by way of Los Angeles.

CML BUILDING Brisbane, Qld 1931 Architect – Hennessy, Hennessy & Co
Now known as the Manor Apartments, this is one of a series of similar CML Buildings across Australia.
This building, notable for its gargoyles, used the beautifully coloured and locally made Benedict stone for its facing.

MAJORCA HOUSE Melbourne. Vic 1928-29 Architect – Harry Norris
At the end of a narrow street leading from Flinders Street Station, an exotic building with an
exotic name by one of Australia's great eclectic architects.

FYSHWICK Castlecrag, Sydney, NSW 1929 Architect – Walter Burley Griffin and Marion Mahony
Specifically designed to play a subordinate role to the natural landscape of Castlecrag,
the Fyshwick house juts out into the bush in the manner of a sandstone outcrop.

WINTHROP HALL University Of Western Australia, Perth, WA 1931 Architect – Alsop & Sayce

An eccentrically proportioned tower and hall which can be viewed from miles in any direction.

The terracotta tiles and limestone walls inspired a 'Mediterranean' look which is seen as perfectly Perth.

WILLIAM JOLLY BRIDGE Brisbane, Qld 1932 Engineer - A E Harding Frew

With its arches echoing the hills of Mt Coot-tha, the William Jolly Bridge was built to carry the weight of burgeoning
Brisbane civic pride, and was opened eleven days after the Sydney Harbour Bridge.

McWHIRTER'S Fortitude Valley, Brisbane, Qld 1931 Architect – Hall & Phillips
A Brisbane landmark known to all, due to its prominent corner location in the Valley and its
unforgettable deco design in brick and terracotta.

SYDNEY HARBOUR BRIDGE Sydney, NSW. 1932 Engineer – J J C Bradfield

As with the Golden Gate, her sister in bridge iconography, the Sydney Harbour Bridge spans her eponymous stretch of
water with a combination of Art Deco aplomb and awe-inspiring structural ingenuity.

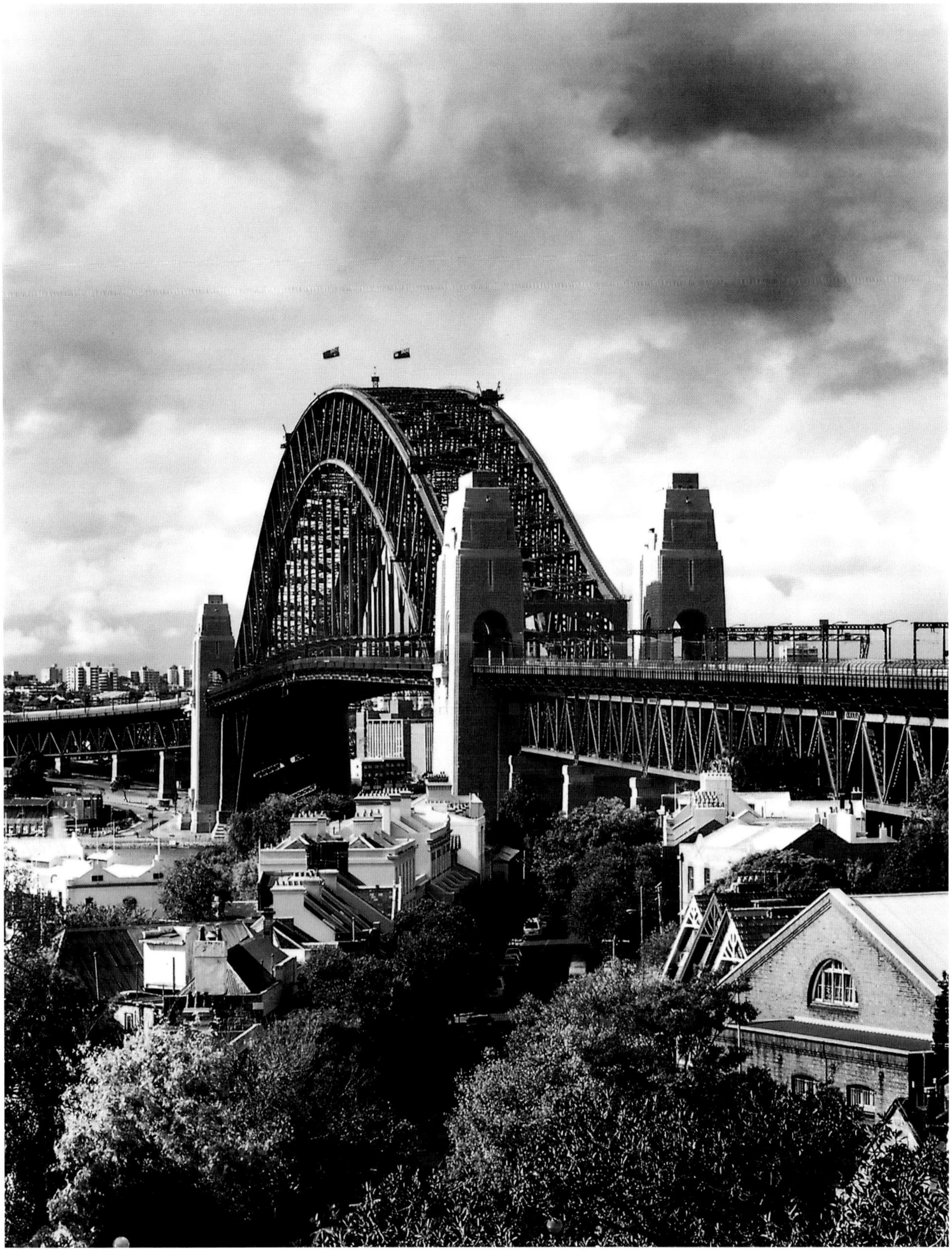

CML BUILDING Sydney, NSW 1936 Architect – Emil Sodersten
Forever twinned with Bruce Dellit in the Art Deco pages of architectural history, Emil Sodersten
reached his zenith with this dynamic corner office block.

ANZAC MEMORIAL Sydney, NSW 1934 Architect – Bruce Dellit

A transcendent shrine sheathed in pink granite, with its monumental massing invigorated
by Raynor Hoff's heroic statues and bas-relief frieze.

MACROBERTSON GIRLS HIGH SCHOOL Melbourne, Vic 1934 Architect – Seabrook and Fildes
In the chronology of Australian architecture, this building gives a sharp shock. Nothing previously seen prepares
one for the straight lines, rectangular volumes, unadorned brickwork, white sills, and complete lack
of ornamentation of our first 'spiritually pure' modern building.

TOWNSVILLE HOSPITAL Townsville, Qld 1935 Architect – Donoghue and Fulton
Wide white verandahs encircling hospitals giving the sunshine cure, provided some of the most photogenic
buildings of the first 'form following function' period.

McPHERSON'S BUILDING Melbourne, Vic 1935 Architect – Stuart Calder
A low slung streamlined version of the International Style in the not the Paris end of Collins Street.

WYLDEFEL GARDENS Potts Point, Sydney, NSW 1936 Architect – W A Crowle and John Brogan
An unexpectedly original and appropriate adaptation of the new German residential architecture to the shores of Sydney Harbour.

HEIDELBERG TOWN HALL Heidelberg, Melbourne, Vic 1938 Architect – Peck and Kempter
The first monumental landmark of the modern architectural forms that arrived in Australia from Copenhagen, Hilversum and Stuttgart.

CENTRAL HOTEL Tamworth, NSW 1938 Architect – V J Davis

A contemporary classic in the country music capital, usually seen by Slim Dusty fans whose
views on critical regionalism in architecture are unknown.

ASHDOWN APARTMENTS Elizabeth Bay, Sydney, NSW 1938 Architect – Aaron Bolot
A white-painted cement-rendered block introducing long horizontal bands of windows,
clean curves and fresh lines to modern apartment living.

AGM FACTORY Waterloo, Sydney, NSW 1940 Architect – Stephenson & Turner and AGM Staff
A large glass brick factory for the makers of glass bricks, who have since moved on, leaving a
landmark to functional expressive design on the road to Sydney's airport.

DELFIN HOUSE Sydney, NSW 1940 Architect – Bruce Dellit
In a final fling of Art Deco sentimentality and symbolism, this massive polished granite arch
is adorned with a frieze entitled 'Sunrise over the Pacific'. Pearl Harbour was bombed the next year.

157

AUSTRALIAN WAR MEMORIAL   Canberra, ACT 1941 Architect – Sodersten and Crust

With its unadorned classical arcades and mighty dome now sadly resembling the architecture of the fascist enemy,
this massive memorial to the fallen was completed during the Second World War. The original design
was produced in 1928 and, although jointly credited, was very much a Sodersten composition.

PICCADILLY THEATRE North Adelaide, SA 1940 Architect – Evans Bruer and Hall with Guy Crick
Featuring chevron windows rising around a sweeping stairway, the Piccadilly Theatre is the most individual
remaining example of the plethora of suburban cinemas which sprang up in the thirties.

STORY BRIDGE Brisbane. Qld 1940 Engineer – J J C Bradfield

As in Sydney, Bradfield designed a landmark bridge with structural complexities and convolutions which
can give drivers a visual experience now referred to as inter-reactive.

GLENUNGA FLATS Armadale, Melbourne Vic 1941 Architect – Romberg & Shaw

Fleeing the Nazis via Switzerland, Frederick Romberg arrived in Australia in 1939 bringing a sophisticated fusion of German Expressionism and Bauhaus craftsmanship. With its use of contrasting materials and geometrically varied detailing, Glenunga displays his virtuosity.

AUDIT HOUSE Darwin, NT 1942 Architect – Beni Burnett
In the now celebrated tropical tradition of houses and gardens becoming integrated living areas,
this largest of all Burnett's Darwin houses is one great room embracing its wonderful garden.

KING GEORGE V HOSPITAL Camperdown, Sydney, NSW 1941 Architect – Stephenson & Turner
With its clean architectural lines, lovely wide balconies accessible to all, and general air of resolute well-ness,
this hospital remains the preferred image of health-care in Australia.

MAIN READING ROOM, STATE LIBRARY OF NSW Sydney, NSW 1939-1942
Government Architect – Cobden Parkes, Design Architect – Samuel Coleman
Something of a stylistic anachronism, with a thirty year old design by Walter Liberty Vernon dusted off, changed in plan
from octagon to rectangle, and shorn of ornament. Despite, or perhaps because of this, the room is a magnificent
space with a balance and harmony set up by the coffered vaulting and the elegant glass ceiling.

A white-painted boxy house without a curve in sight, save for three porthole windows in the front door, dropped into the gumtrees of the Australian bush. Inappropriate, discordant, ridiculous, belongs on a street corner in Utrecht? Well, no, the modernist abstract geometry and clean white lines of the Russell Ellis house on the slopes of the Adelaide Hills sit beautifully in the tangled willfulness of the native bushland. This juxtaposition of simple pristine geometric houses with rugged bushland was first seen at Wahroonga, on Sydney's North Shore, where Harry Seidler designed three houses for his family in an uncompromising fashion, borrowing from Breuer and delivering Mondrian to the bush. Climatic inappropriateness notwithstanding, the freshness and vitality of these houses actually enhanced awareness of the rugged landscape, providing a simple deferential frame of reference in the untamed bushland.

Further inventive approaches to the integration of houses with the unyielding local terrain led to an exciting, romantic, and eventually highly-principled local architecture. Firstly Peter Muller, and then Bruce Rickard, adopted an organic approach to building low-slung spreading houses on Sydney's North Shore, which embraced and attempted to harmonize with the rocky bushland. The 'Sydney School' followed, with architects flagging a return to crafted vernacular structure with the use of rough brickwork, dark-stained timber, and an honest empathy with bushland sites.

Australian architecture soared in the post-war period, as individual architects found endless opportunities for expression and experimentation in the baby-booming suburbs. The Melbourne heroes of Grounds, Boyd and McIntyre became obsessed with the potential of geometric trickery, and in their best moments, such as Peter McIntyre's house at Kew, created iconic structures that can obliterate architectural ennui instantly. Perhaps the most original and expressive work in Australia's architectural history is to be found at this time - the house by Stan Symonds at Seaforth, those by Hugh Buhrich at Castlecrag and Jean Fombertaux at Lindfield, the best buildings by James Birrell in Brisbane, Neville Gruzman's peerless house at Middle Cove, and Eddie Oribin's inventive singularity in Northern Queensland. These individual architects, often migrants, were working outside the mainstream (both critically and commercially) and displayed the occasional flicker of genius.

Within the mainstream, things weren't too bad either. Harry Seidler's Australia Square Tower in Sydney remains one of the world's most elegantly resolved skyscrapers. The ICI Building in Melbourne, and the Qantas Building in Sydney's Chifley Square are beautiful examples of sheer glass-walled luminescence. Sadly, Australia's other great skyscraper from the sixties, Ken Woolley's State Office Block in Sydney was demolished in 1998. The jewel in the crown, of course, is the Sydney Opera House, an astonishing manifestation of triumphant imagination and spirit.

ADELAIDE HIGH SCHOOL Adelaide. SA 1947 Architect – Fitzgerald & Brogan
Standing alone on Adelaide's grassy sward, an anomalous monument to thirties streamlined brick and glass architecture.

WYLDE STREET APARTMENTS Potts Point, Sydney, NSW 1951 Architect – Aaron Bolot

An articulate and discreetly modulated semi-circular facade following the curve of the road leading up to Kings Cross from Garden Island.

STANHILL APARTMENTS   Melbourne, Vic 1948 Architect – Romberg & Shaw
A *tour de force* from Frederick Romberg, a masterpiece of plastic expression in concrete and glass, that
has a different personality and metaphorical value for each elevational view. Scratch the
surface of any architectural historian, and you'll find that this is their favourite building.

ROSE SEIDLER HOUSE Wahroonga, Sydney, NSW 1950 Architect – Harry Seidler

The unrivalled architectural talent and self-conviction of the Viennese-born Harry Seidler arrived in Australia shortly after World War II. This house for mother in the bush of Sydney's North Shore introduced an urbanity and savoir-faire much needed by local architecture after the lost years of the war.

MARCUS SEIDLER HOUSE Wahroonga, Sydney, NSW 1951 Architect – Harry Seidler
The third house in the Seidler family compound, featuring a mural by Harry himself.

173

WRIGHT HOUSE Springfield, Adelaide, SA 1952 Architect – Russell Ellis
Still occupied by the original owner, the Wright house stands pristine and assured, a modern gem
in the leafy suburban foothills of the Mt Lofty Ranges.

HILL STREET HOUSE Toorak, Melbourne, Vic 1954 Architect – Roy Grounds
A square house with a circular central courtyard designed for his own use by Roy Grounds, a prolific and
influential architect with an abiding love for platonic forms and geometric juxtaposition.

AUDETTE HOUSE Castlecrag, Sydney, NSW 1953 Architect – Peter Muller

An early example of the organic domestic work, influenced by Japanese and contemporary American architecture, produced on Sydney's
North Shore in the fifties by Peter Muller, Bruce Rickard, and Neville Gruzman.

BRETT HOUSE Toorak, Melbourne, Vic 1955 Architect – Robin Boyd

A restrained and elegant essay in the Georgian style by an architect renowned for his varied and ingenious Melbourne houses, most of which have sadly deteriorated or disappeared.

McINTYRE HOUSE Kew, Melbourne, Vic 1954 Architect – Peter & Dione McIntyre
Perfectly poised on a steep riverbank in Kew, and looking like an amusement ride in an architectural theme park, this
cantilevered structure supported by an A-frame tower remains a vision splendid of inventive imaginative design.

WILSON HALL University of Melbourne, Parkville, Vic 1956 Architect – Bates Smart McCutcheon
Designed by Oswald McCutcheon and clad internally with Swedish birch, Wilson Hall must have an unsettling
effect on students doing their exams, rather like sitting inside a giant Globite school-case.
For light relief they could try deciphering Douglas Annand's quixotic mural.

GRUZMAN HOUSE Darling Point, Sydney, NSW 1958 Architect – Neville Gruzman

Containing a living room described by Jørn Utzon as Australia's finest, Neville Gruzman's beautifully crafted house winds around its garden
with low maple ceilings and flowing spaces adapted from traditional Japanese architecture.

QANTAS BUILDING Sydney, NSW 1957 Architect – Rudder Littlemore & Rudder
A curved green-glass wall framed with sandstone, bringing a sweeping brightness to the
narrow angular canyons of Sydney's financial district.

ICI BUILDING Melbourne, Vic 1960 Architect – Bates Smart McCutcheon
Australia's most beautiful glass skyscraper, with a sheer unblemished skin of blue glass, a
simple elegant base and a dramatic position on Melbourne's Eastern Hill.

MYER MUSIC BOWL Melbourne, Vic 1959 Architect – Yuncken Freeman

The only surviving large structure from the free-willed experimentation in Melbourne architecture that flourished in the years following the war. The idea of a vast canopy suspended from two slender masts was conceived by a young architect, Barry Patten, and made possible by structural engineer Bill Irwin.

ACADEMY OF SCIENCE Canberra. ACT 1959 Architect – Roy Grounds
Emblematic of Australian architecture during the sixties — every schoolkid had a picture of the Academy of Science on their
standard issue wooden ruler. The structure is a fanciful elaboration of Roy Grounds' obsession
with circles, and most appropriate for the rounded contours of Canberra.

185

TOOWONG LIBRARY Toowong, Brisbane, Qld 1959 Architect – James Birrell

A spinning top sitting on a bend of Coronation Drive, Toowong Library is characteristic of the exuberant Brisbane buildings of James Birrell who, at the time, was probably Australia's most spirited and inventive designer.

HALE SCHOOL MEMORIAL HALL Wembley, Perth, WA 1961 Architect – Marshall Clifton with Anthony Brand
A suburban Perth landmark to the sculpted concrete architecture inspired by the
late work of Le Corbusier and labelled, rather unsympathetically, as 'brutalism'.

DELBRIDGE HOUSE Eaglemont, Melbourne. Vic 1960
A wonderfully elegant house floating above its Heidelberg hillside site, designed by the builder owner
with the assistance of structural engineer, Emery Balint.

LINER HOUSE Sydney, NSW 1961 Architect – Bunning & Madden
A delicate presence in a streetscape consisting of heavy sandstone buildings,
with a Douglas Annand sculpture running the length of the mezzanine floor.

TORBRECK Highgate Hill, Brisbane, Qld 1961 Architect – Job & Froud
An uncompromising modernist apartment block standing proud on the South Brisbane hill
otherwise covered with poinciana, frangipani, palm trees and weatherboard cottages.

190

ANZ BANK (Previously E S & A) Canberra, ACT 1961 Architect – Stuart McIntosh
A four storey baklava in the heart of Canberra by Stuart McIntosh, whose idiosyncratic designs for the E S & A Bank
in the late fifties and early sixties enliven many commercial precincts across Australia.

AUSWILD HOUSE Rose Bay, Sydney, NSW 1961 Architect – Ken Willoughby

Simon Templar's harbourside home, a crazy paving house redolent of sixties nowness, canapés on the patio, and who was that masked man?

WOOLLEY HOUSE Mosman, Sydney, NSW 1962 Architect – Ken Woolley
Stepping down a densely vegetated hillside, Ken Woolley's moody evocative house is the
epitome of the tree-hugging vernacular architecture now known as the Sydney School.

193

ST ANDREW'S Innisfail, Qld 1961 Architect – Eddie Oribin

The isoscelean masterpiece of an ever-resourceful maverick architect.

HOLLAND HOUSE Middle Cove, Sydney, NSW 1962
Architect – Neville Gruzman
A house for a pair of lovebirds perched on a cliff,
displaying Neville Gruzman's unrivalled gift for
architectural articulation combined with theatrical flair.

ORIBIN STUDIO Cairns, Qld 1963 Architect – Eddie Oribin
A studio for one painted in cardinal red, tucked away in the myrtle green of the Cairns rainforest. Happy colours.

197

MICHEL HOUSE Adelaide, SA 1964 Architect – Peter Muller
Leaving Fallingwater well behind, this 'L' shaped pavilion house presages Muller's sublime designs for Balinese resort hotels.

C B ALEXANDER COLLEGE Tocal, NSW 1964 Architect – Ian McKay and Philip Cox
The revival of the Australian vernacular tradition as a reaction to prevailing modernist orthodoxy, reached its zenith
on a hilltop in the Hunter Valley, with joinery details inspired by a neighbouring Edmund Blacket barn.

MIRRABOOKA Castle Hill, Sydney, NSW 1964 Architect – Bruce Rickard

Adopting Japanese and American principles of floating planes and fluid space, Mirrabooka is a
perfectly preserved specimen of the organic architecture which flowered in the Sydney bush.

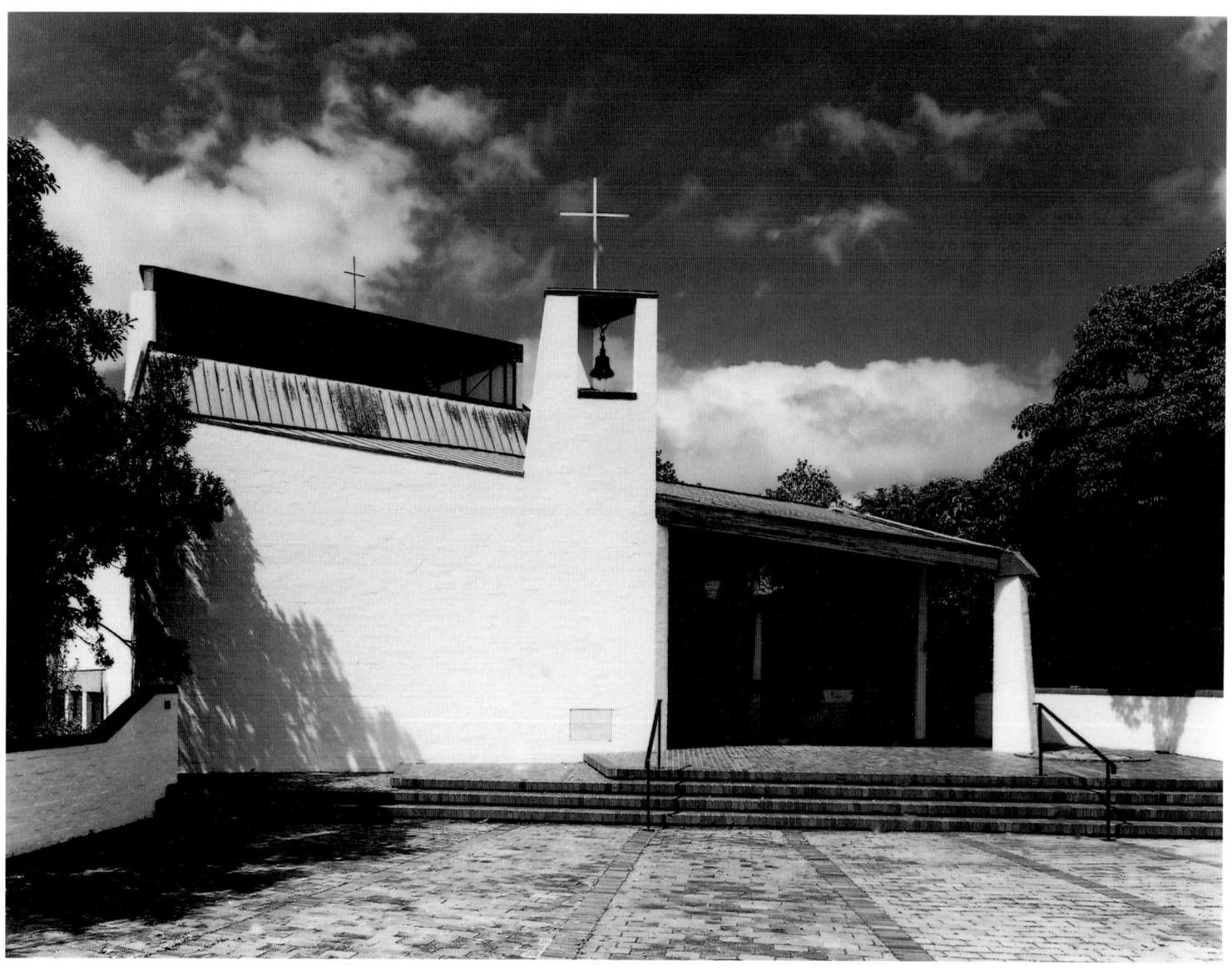

WENTWORTH CHAPEL Vaucluse, Sydney, NSW 1965 Architect – Don Gazzard
A celebrated combination of Greek island whitewashed forms with the prevailing vernacular
architecture of the Sydney School. A pilgrimage chapel for architectural tourists.

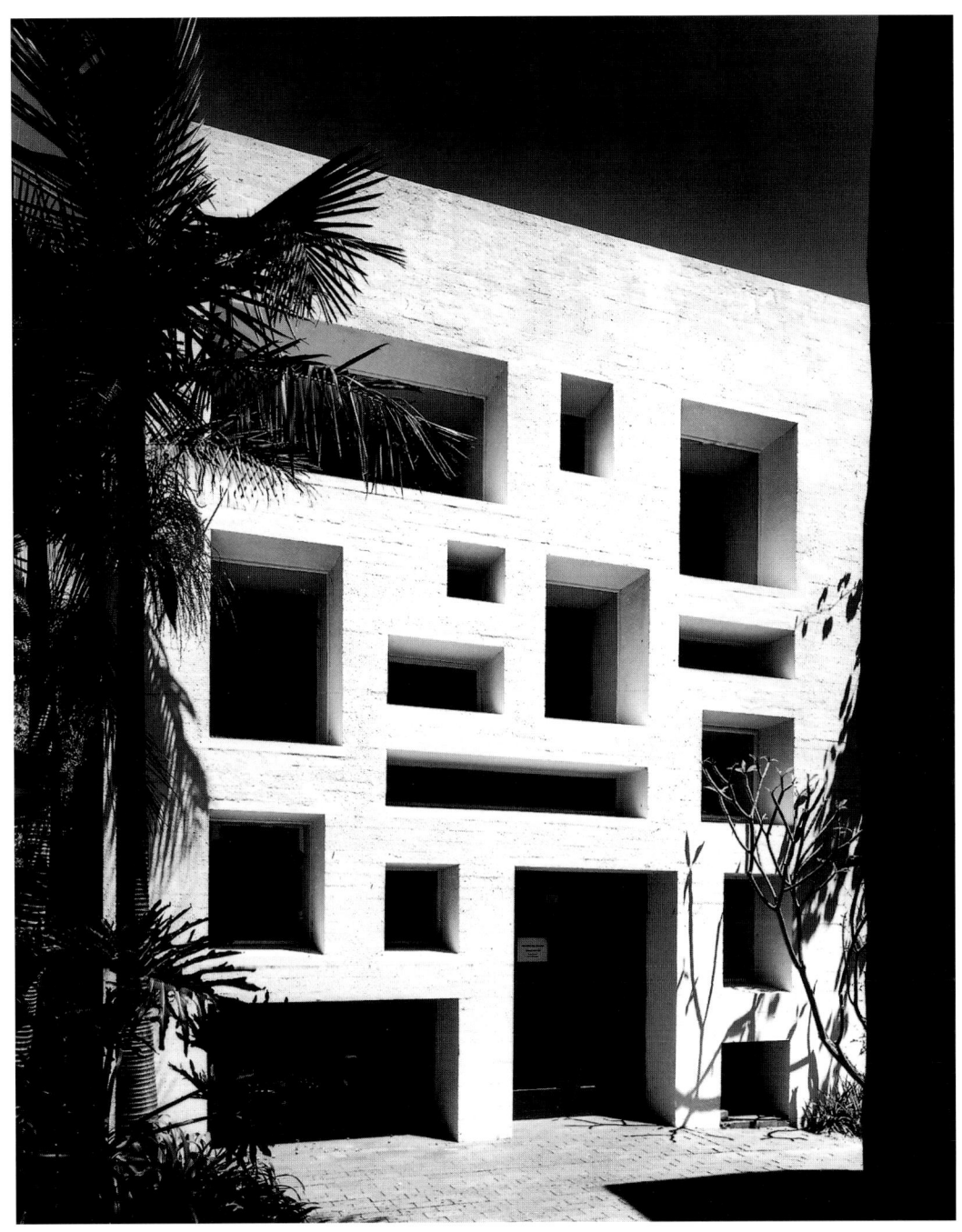

BROADWAY SHOWROOM Nedlands, Perth, WA 1964 Architect – Julius Elischer

Mondrian chiselled out of a whitewashed brick wall, built as a showroom for modern furniture.

MENZIES COLLEGE Bundoora, Melbourne, Vic 1967 Architect – Robin Boyd

Designed late in Robin Boyd's career, Menzies College is a metabolist-brutalist hybrid which has aged remarkably well, suggesting that
Boyd's urbane and eclectic talents warranted a larger stage and a wider audience.

POLISH WAR MEMORIAL CHAPEL Marayong, Sydney, NSW 1966 Architect – Michael Dysart

Here's the church and here's the steeple, open the doors and here are the people.

AUSTRALIA SQUARE Sydney, NSW 1967 Architect – Harry Seidler
A monument to oxymoronic appellation, this circular tower is Australia's finest tall building, one that should be seen with Milan's Pirelli Building, and the Lake Point Tower in Chicago as a perfect resolution of rational geometry, structural ingenuity and heroic form.

SCHUCHARD HOUSE Seaforth, Sydney, NSW 1967 Architect – Stan Symonds
The perfect house for a party, designed in the style now referred to as 'futuristic'.

MUSEUM OF MODERN ART AT HEIDE Bulleen, Melbourne, Vic 1968 Architect – McGlashan & Everist

A limestone art gallery with sun-filled courtyards and double height rooms, masquerading as a house for John and
Sunday Reed, who retreated to the original cottage next door in 1980.

207

TOWER HILL NATURAL HISTORY CENTRE Koroit, Vic 1963-70 Architect – Robin Boyd

A mushroom built from stone and wood in the beautiful flooded crater of Tower Hill. The mushroom
metaphor is continued inside, with thin curved timber trusses radiating from a thick stone stalk.

208

FOMBERTAUX HOUSE Lindfield, Sydney, NSW 1972 Architect – J G Fombertaux
One of the myriad unique interpretations of modernist house architecture on Sydney's North Shore,
the architects frequently being European migrants building their new homes in the bush.

209

SYDNEY OPERA HOUSE Bennelong Point, Sydney, NSW 1973 Architect – Jørn Utzon

Unchallenged as the architectural wonder of the twentieth century, an astounding manifestation of triumphant imagination and spirit.

BUHRICH HOUSE Castlecrag, Sydney, NSW 1972 Architect – Hugh Buhrich
A wonderful tactile room with a moulded timber ceiling that has quickly become architectural legend.

ADDISON HOUSE Taringa, Brisbane, Qld 1975 Architect – Rex Addison

A friendly inviting house nestling comfortably in the verdant luxuriance of Brisbane's hillside suburbs.

DIANELLA HEIGHTS HOUSE Perth, WA 1977 Architect – Iwan Iwanoff
A dream home in the Mayan style, built from Besser blocks and designed by the
Bulgarian Iwanoff whose eccentric visions enliven Perth's endless sandy suburbs.

HIGH COURT Canberra, ACT 1980 Architect – Edwards Madigan Torzillo & Briggs

An austere abstracted concrete box, noticeably devoid of human scale. A metaphor for supreme jurisprudence.

214

The northern beach suburbs of Sydney can be impossibly beautiful, being variously referred to as 'La La Land', and 'Gods Own Country'. One of these suburbs, having ingenuously named itself Avalon, has the surf on one side and the protected bays of Pittwater on the other. Sitting amongst the gums on the slope running down to Pittwater is a beautifully crafted, jewel-like pavilion, as if one of those lanterns that mark the path in a Balinese resort hotel took one of Alice's pills, and grew and grew. This house by Peter Stutchbury, actually built by the architect and the owner, is a lyrical example of the application and implementation of highly principled design and construction. It is a spirited and sophisticated architectural exercise with oriental allusions, indigenous compatibility and a refined vernacular construction technique.

Architects such as Glenn Murcutt, Rick Leplastrier, Gabriel Poole, the Clares, Rex Addison, Russell Hall, and Troppo, had picked up on the development of appropriate vernacular architecture in Australia and gave it a spiritual and pragmatic profundity. An infectious uplifting philosophy evolved - respecting and admiring the Aboriginal empathy with the land, drawing on the craftsmanship and romantic rugged styling of the Sydney School, and appropriating the tropical architecture of New Guinea and Indonesia. The architecture and the architects have become justly celebrated, as much for the honesty of architectural intention and function, as for the aesthetic and sculptural qualities of the houses and occasional public buildings. The best of these practitioners are architecturally erudite (historically and stylistically) and this knowledge and urbanity permeates their work.

There was, however, more to Australian architecture after 1980 than romantic houses in the bush, and Melbourne was the stage for dramatic architectural hyperbole that periodically manifested itself in spectacular structure. The most prolific and assured work was by Denton Corker Marshall, and the most provocative, polemical, and colourful by Peter Corrigan. Psychedelic stylists such as Ashton Raggatt & McDougall, and Wood Marsh have produced architectonically charged landmarks to expressionist rhetoric and foppish indulgence. Most illuminating and uplifting is the oeuvre of Nonda Katsalidis which mixes dynamic and unexpected material composition with a cross-cultural eclecticism.

Iconic public architecture flourished across Australia in the wake of the Sydney Opera House. The most celebrated and stylistically emphatic practitioner has been Philip Cox, while Daryl Jackson and Lawrence Nield applied a more pluralist and architecturally referential approach. Commercial building design has withered generally since the sixties, with 'nothing succeeds like excess' being the depressing visual aphorism for the cities. Melbourne has been the honourable and virtuous exception, with a continuing series of skyscrapers that enhance rather than degrade.

The tradition of brilliant maverick architects continues, now with considerable critical acclaim - uncompromising, dogmatic and highly principled architects thrive. The magic and whimsy of Neil Durbach , the sculptural brilliance of Nonda Katsalidis and the bushland masterpieces of lightweight construction by Poole and Murcutt, are an Australian antidote to universal corporate banality

CARRUTHERS HOUSE Mt Irvine, NSW 1980 Architect – Glenn Murcutt
A simple farmhouse, an elegant shed, and a polemical re-establishment of traditional local architecture.

GLOSTER HOUSE Noosa Heads, Qld 1984 Architect – Gabriel Poole with Michael Gloster
Designed in conjunction with his client, architect turned local activist Michael Gloster, this house
utilizes Gabriel Poole's quadropod construction system and demonstrates his now renowned
combination of lightweight materials, angular composition, and ecological awareness.

HALL HOUSE Wilston, Brisbane, Qld 1985 Architect – Russell Hall

Let down your hair. Rapunzel's tower in the northern Brisbane suburbs is reminiscent in spirit
of such earlier urban landmarks as Carclew (page 93) and the Range Convent (page 112).

HENWOOD HOUSE Paddington, Sydney, NSW 1985 Architect – Lewin Tzannes
An etched classical facade in ornamental Paddington, so restrained that it passes unnoticed
by non-architects who probably think that it's an old Regency terrace with a new paint job.

OVERSEAS PASSENGER TERMINAL Circular Quay, Sydney, NSW 1987 Architect – Lawrence Nield and Partners
A deconstruction and reconfiguration of a near-redundant 1950s terminal building, now looking like an
early scheme for the battleship Potemkin, or the workings of a clockwork engine.

TUSCULUM Potts Point, Sydney, NSW 1988 Architect – Harry Levine & Neil Durbach
A mulberry coloured extension to a verandahed Verge villa which frames fragmented views of
the architectonically charged spaces of the new building.

SYDNEY FOOTBALL STADIUM Paddington, Sydney, NSW 1988 Architect – Philip Cox Richardson Taylor & Partners

A singular inspired elliptical vision translated into a swooping swirling structure adorning Sydney's eastern suburbs.

223

SYDNEY EXHIBITION CENTRE Darling Harbour, Sydney, NSW 1988 Architect – Philip Cox Richardson Taylor & Partners
Philip Cox's adaptation of steel design and advanced structural technology produced a graceful nautically-inspired architecture
now symbolic of the time that Japanese tour group operators discovered the harbour city and made it their own.

AUSTRALIAN PARLIAMENT HOUSE Canberra, ACT 1988 Architect – Mitchell Giurgola Thorp
Completing Walter Burley Griffin's capital plan is a vast grass-covered bunker containing expensive furniture
and polished marble. Probably Australia's largest building, but one that doesn't want to be seen.

RIVERSIDE PLACE Brisbane, Qld 1988 Architect – Harry Seidler
One of a series of similar simultaneous Seidler towers (others in Sydney, Perth and Melbourne), featuring polished grey granite
facing, projecting louvres, monumental ground-level sculpting and an abstract curved plan varying from city to city.

120 AND 101 COLLINS STREET Melbourne, Vic 1991 and 1990
Architect – 120 Collins – Daryl Jackson & Hassell   101 Collins - Denton Corker Marshall
Towering manifestations of corporate pride and optimism built just in time for the recession.
If this sounds familiar, substitute mercantile for corporate and refer back to 1891.

ARGUS CENTRE Melbourne, Vic 1991 Architect – Nonda Katsalidis with Axia Pty Ltd
A dramatic disrhythmic assemblage of conflicting lines and contrasting materials
demonstrating the singular skills of Nonda Katsalidis.

GREAT SOUTHERN STAND Melbourne Cricket Ground, Jolimont, Vic 1990
Architect – Daryl Jackson with Tomkins, Shaw & Evans
When packed with footy fans, the true symbol of the great southern city. This massive grandstand shows off
Daryl Jackson's inimitable combination of monumental forms and elegant structure.

MAPLETON HOUSE Sunshine Coast, Qld 1991 Architect – Rick Leplastrier

Only phenomenological intervention could disturb the tranquility of this house in the forest by
an architect who specializes in harnessing spiritual requirements to environmental concerns.

DONE HOUSE Balmoral, Sydney, NSW 1992 Architect – Glenn Murcutt
The other side of Glenn Murcutt. Celebrated for his corrugated 'sheds' in the bush, this house in a
harbourside suburb is an assured and elegant essay in the classical Miesian style.

STOKES STREET HOUSE Darwin, NT 1992 Architect – Troppo

A gabled house reminiscent of an outback pub, by a Darwin partnership whose colourful and cheeky advocacy
of vernacular tropical architecture should not conceal their sophisticated and referential formal design skills.

ISRAEL HOUSE Avalon, Sydney, NSW 1992 Architect – Peter Stutchbury

With its curved roof faithfully describing the arc of the setting sun, this hillside house on Sydney's northern
beaches has a distinctly oriental look. An afternoon teahouse maybe, or a temple to surfism.

CLARE HOUSE Buderim, Sunshine Coast, Qld 1992 Architect – Lindsay & Kerry Clare
A literally uplifting family home for the Clares, whose spirited and articulate use
of lightweight steel and timber symbolizes recent coastal architecture.

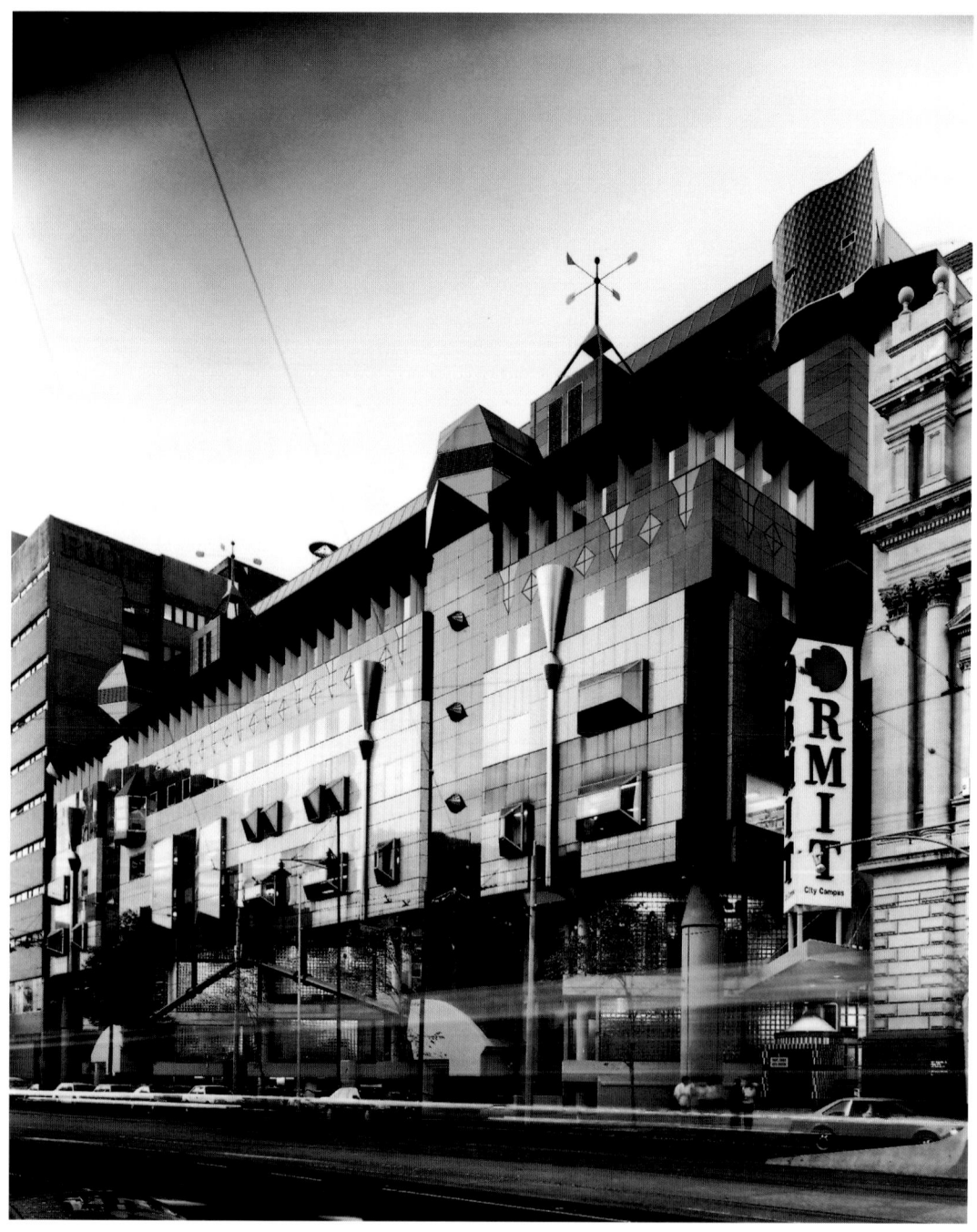

RMIT BUILDING 8 Melbourne, Vic 1994 Architect – Edmond Corrigan with Demaine Partnership
Antonio Gaudi meets Darth Vader in a spectacular reworking of a seventies concrete block,
by an architect, Peter Corrigan, whose polemic and performance has been colourful and varied.

STOREY HALL Melbourne, Vic 1995 Architect – Ashton Raggatt McDougall with Allom Lovell Associates
An hallucinogenic prismatic lime-green experience. Architectural historians will fidget
with this one. Expect an outburst of excitement every twenty years or so.

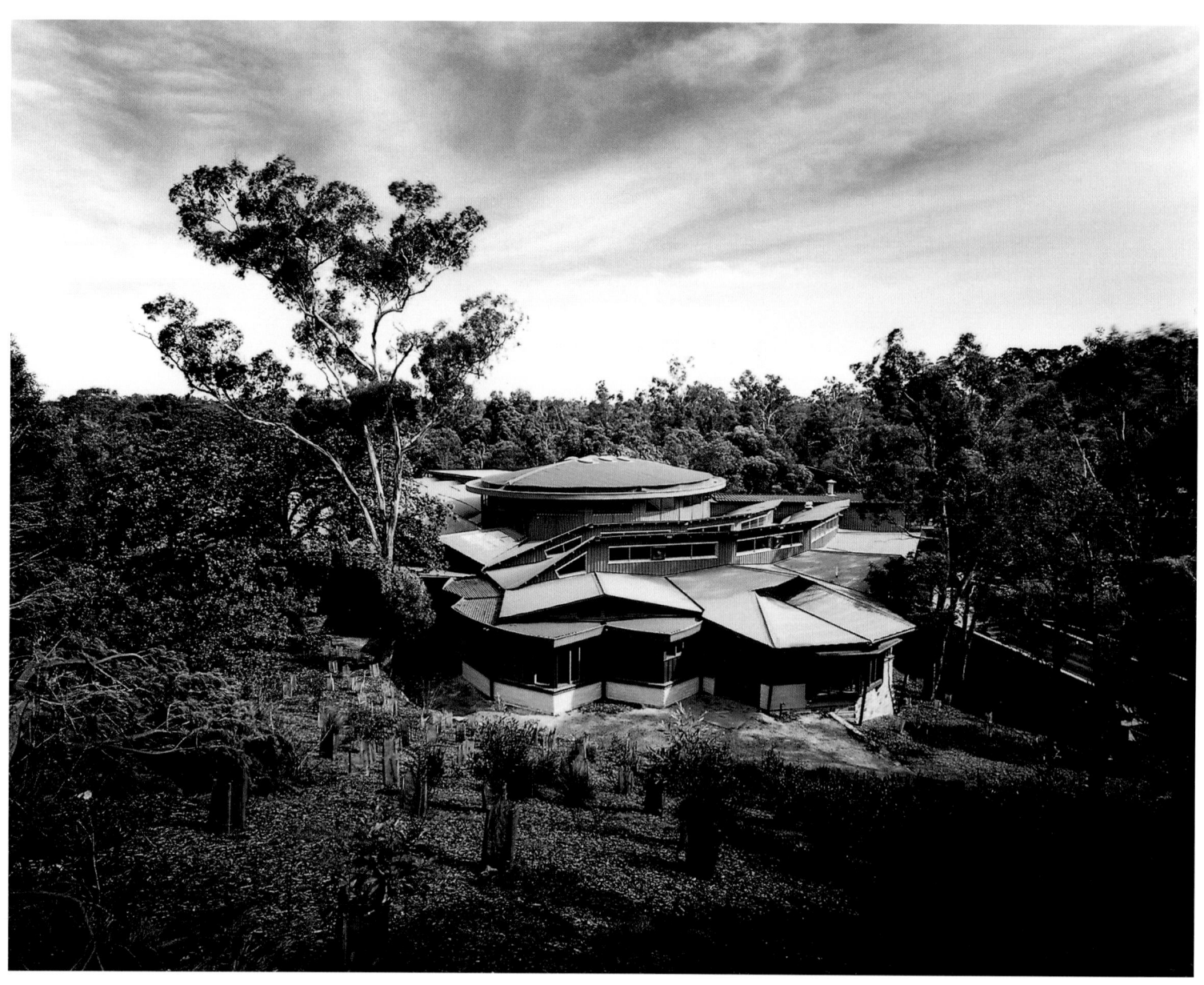

ELTHAM LIBRARY Eltham, Melbourne, Vic 1994 Architect – Greg Burgess
Also known for two shingled snakes near Uluru and a corrugated goanna in the Grampians, the vernacular
expressionism of Greg Burgess sits snugly in the alternative lifestyle pocket of outer Melbourne.

LAKE WEYBA HOUSE Sunshine Coast, Qld 1996 Architect – Gabriel Poole

Three linked skillion pavilions demonstrating the refinement of Poole's subliminal skill and flair.

SUNSHINE COAST UNIVERSITY LIBRARY Maroochydore, Qld 1996 Architect – John Mainwaring & Lawrence Nield

With its great crustacean form stalking the campus, this university library is a monument to the expressive
use of lightweight steel and timber popularly known as the 'Sunshine Coast' school of architecture.

MELBOURNE TERRACES Melbourne, Vic 1994 Architect – Nonda Katsalidis
Overlooking the markets in a city with a large number of Greek and Italian migrants, a muscular sculpted apartment
block in the style of the less than romantic suburbs of Mediterranean cities.

MELBOURNE EXHIBITION CENTRE
Melbourne, Vic 1996 Architect – Denton Corker Marshall
A pristine building from a firm whose work epitomises the past decade of
Melbourne architectural revitalization with a combination of dramatic
geometry, selective historicism and meticulous detailing.

242

GOVERNOR MACQUARIE TOWER Sydney, NSW 1995 Architect – Denton Corker Marshall
A beautifully detailed and appropriately intimidating lift lobby for humble citizens summoned
by the corporate lawyers and government departments up above.

DEAKIN UNIVERSITY BUILDINGS Burwood, Melbourne, Vic 1997 Architect – Wood Marsh with Pels Innes Neilson & Kosloff

A radiating assemblage of buildings notable for their reverential and referential use of modernist materials and forms.

DROGA APARTMENT Surry Hills, Sydney, NSW 1997 Architect – Durbach Block
A zinc-clad call from the rooftops, proclaiming the architectural possibilities of inner-city regeneration.

SILO APARTMENTS Richmond, Melbourne, Vic 1997 Architect – Nonda Katsalidis
An inventive and romantic addition in the form of a ship's prow to an existing silo building. On each floor the prow
provides the view and the entertainment, while the four round rooms of the silo are where people do what they have to do.

GODSELL HOUSE Kew, Melbourne, Vic 1997 Architect – Sean Godsell
A rusting cage teetering on a sculpted rock. A machine for living in, particularly if you're an architect.

ADDISON STUDIO Taringa, Brisbane, Qld 1998 Architect – Rex Addison

Undaunted by ephemeral stylistic propinquity, the sparkle and translucence of the
architect's own studio brings a green gully to life.

248

OLYMPIC PARK RAILWAY STATION Homebush Bay, Sydney, NSW 1998 Architect – Hassell
In the shape of a stainless-steel caterpillar inching its way across the Homebush plain, the Olympic
Park Railway Station is a seductive integration of imaginative design and technological precision.

index

253

bibliography

Historic Towns of Australia. Philip Cox and Wesley Stacey.
  Lansdowne Press 1973
A Spirit of Progress. Art Deco Architecture in Australia. Patrick van
  Daele and Roy Lumby. Craftsman House 1997
Queensland Architects of the 19th Century. Donald Watson and
  Judith McKay. Queensland Museum 1994
Leslie Wilkinson. Max Dupain, Peter Johnson, George Molnar,
  David Wilkinson. Valdon Publishing 1982
Historic Court Houses of New South Wales. Peter Bridges. Hale and
  Iremonger 1986
Historic Public Buildings of Australia, Volume Two. Australian
  Council of National Trusts. Cassell 1971
Historic Buildings of Australia, Volume One. Australian Council of
  National Trusts. Cassell 1977
*Towards the Dawn, Federation Architecture in Australia,
  1890 - 1915.* Trevor Howells and Michael Nicholson.
  Hale & Iremonger 1989
Identifying Australian Architecture. Richard Apperly, Robert Irving,
  and Peter Reynolds. Angus & Robertson 1989
Architecture Newcastle. Barry Maitland and David Stafford.
  RAIA (Newcastle Division) 1997
Sydney Architecture. Graham Jahn. The Watermark Press 1997
Architects of Australia. Edited by Howard Tanner. MacMillan 1981
Old Continent, New Building. Edited by Leon Paroissien and
  Michael Griggs. David Ell Press 1983
Australian Houses of the Forties and Fifties. Peter Cuffley.
  Five Mile Press 1993
Gabriel Poole. Space in Which the Soul Can Play. Bruce Walker.
  Visionary Press 1998
Birrell. Work From the Office of James Birrell. Edited by Andrew
  Wilson and John McArthur. NMBW Publications 1997
Heroic Melbourne. Architecture of the 1950s. Norman Day.
  RMIT Publications 1995
Melbourne Architecture. Philip Goad. The Watermark Press 1999
Looking Around Perth. Ian Molyneux. Wescolour Press in
  association with the Western Australian Chapter of RAIA 1981
B Architectural Magazine 1996 Edition 52

254

acknowledgements

I would like to thank the following people for their specific
suggestions and advice in the preparation of this book.

Bruce Eeles for his encyclopaedic knowledge of Australian
architectural history, and for his continual assessment of the
direction and content of the book;
Alice Hampson who shared her extensive knowledge of
Queensland architecture;
Philip Goad for his Victorian erudition and enthusiasm;
Fiona Gardiner for her comprehensive and detailed information on
Queensland's heritage buildings;
Lindsay Clare who provided me with the perfect guide to the
Sunshine Coast;
Graham Jahn and Ann-Elise Hampton for their research and
collaboration in Sydney; and
Adrian Welke who showed me which way was up in Darwin.

I am also grateful to **Davina Jackson, Heidi Dokulil, Kate Stewart,
Chris Johnson, Don Watson, Philip Cox, Jackie Urford** and **Kathy
Trelease** for their help and encouragement. Likewise to **Rex and
Susan Addison** for their Brisbane bed and breakfast, and to **Libby
Guj** for a couch in Cottesloe.

PEE WEES AT THE POINT Darwin, NT 1998 Architect - Troppo